Finally I Like Myself

MY CLIMB FROM SELF-DOUBT TO SELF-CONFIDENCE

Joseph Skillin

NEW HARBOR PRESS

RAPID CITY, SD

Skillin/New Harbor Press
1601 Mt. Rushmore Rd, Ste 3288
Rapid City, SD 57701
www.NewHarborPress.com

Ordering Information:
Quantity sales. Special discounts are available on quantity purchases by corporations, associations, and others. For details, contact the "Special Sales Department" at the address above.

Finally I Like Myself / Joseph Skillin. -- 1st ed.
ISBN 978-1-63357-385-7

To Penny, who still watches over me and guides me.

To my children, Jim, Jill and Emily, whose love I cherish, whom I love deeply.

Contents

PREFACE

WHILE THIS BOOK IS not a typical self-improvement hand-book, it offers a lot to learn about self-confidence. It is the story of my own struggles with self-doubt while desperately grasping for that illusive personal calm we find in self-confidence. It took me many years into adulthood before I could say, "Finally I like myself."

For all of us, life is a constant wrestling match between self-doubt and self-confidence. I tell my story in the hope that it will help you better understand that wrestling match and come to the point where you declare self-confidence the uncontested winner.

ACKNOWLEDGMENTS

FINALLY, I WAS ABLE to write this book thanks to several people who have greatly influenced my sense of confidence.....

First, Jesus. The miracle worker, always forgiving and encouraging, always saying I am special and magnificent. The seed of Self-confidence.

To Brené Brown. Her pattern of: *I am good enough, I belong, I should be good to myself, I am worthy.* Her words have inspired me. She has gathered so many good and important thoughts and expressed them so clearly that they have profoundly influenced my thinking about Self-confidence.

Likewise John Boyle, founder of the Omega Seminar. Over many years, attendees were impressed by the seminar but I was *inspired* by it! This book is so much a reflection of Omega.

INTRODUCTION

I FEEL VERY SELF-CONFIDENT these days. Mostly, I appear and act with confidence. My nephew says I radiate it. Some read it as cocky or conceit. Without denying that these two reside in me, I think mostly that my nephew is correct -- what I have and portray is honest confidence, self-confidence. I have trust in myself.

I wasn't always this way. As a child, although I grew up in a loving family, my childhood dominant feeling was not self-confidence, but self-doubt. Everyone has doubts. As adults, we hold doubts about what we can do, how we present ourselves, what people think of us. We were not born with self-doubt. The philosophers say we start life as a "tabula rasa", a blank page. They state that individuals are born without built-in mental content, and, therefore all knowledge comes from experience or perception. Self-doubt is placed upon us through our early experiences and by what we perceive from them. When Mother gave me a teething ring and then neglected me for what seemed like forever, I may have perceived that I was not as special as I thought I was. An impression, a mark of self-doubt on my *tabula rasa*. Or when I was four and my dad claimed, "You're a bad boy!", I ramped up some serious self-doubt. And so it goes. While we were not born with self-doubt, influential people prompted us to have serious doubts about ourselves from a very young age. Soon I'll tell you some stories about my own experiences and perceptions that had me doubting myself at a very early age.

How I morphed from that self-doubt to self-confidence is the story of this book, my story, the decades of slow progression that eventually turned negative feelings into positive feelings. In some ways my story is ordinary. Thousands of people struggle to overcome self-doubt and live confident, fulfilling lives. So can you.

I'm not a doctor or psychologist. I tell my personal story with the simple hope that my road might inspire just one person, you, to change self-doubt into self-confidence. You put this book in your hands because something in the title clicked with you. Perhaps you doubt yourself too much. Maybe you have that debilitating feeling that you're not worthy, not good enough. Maybe you look at your friends and feel, "I can't really compete with them. I don't really belong in this crowd." Perhaps there is a strong and persistent jealousy that you have carried for years, jealous of a sibling, an old friend, a work associate. Before increasing your self-confidence significantly, you need to admit your self-doubts. You don't have to understand fully their genesis or why they seem to persist, creeping across your soul like a vine, wrapping you in their persistence. All you need do is admit that they exist. If you can clearly identify them, that is a plus, a good start.

You can change. On your own or with professional help doesn't matter. For years, I didn't like myself. Now, finally I like myself. I trust myself. I am comfortable with myself. If I have been able to change, so can you. It took me years. But with support and help and the tools available today, you can change quickly. Gradually, but relatively quickly. You can start to feel better about yourself in one to two months if you work at it. It's a process, so time and dedication are necessary. If you use the tools I present, you'll see results, you'll change. You'll gradually feel better and better about yourself, you'll gradually become more and more self-confident. You'll significantly stifle those feelings of not being worthy or not belonging. You are worthy. You are special. You belong. Be confident.

Life is a constant wrestling match between self-doubt and self-confidence. I lived that match for almost 50 years before self-confidence became the uncontested winner. This is my personal story, my own experience and observations. Fortunately it's a positive experience, changing from self-doubt to self-confidence.

Let's start where I started – with self-doubt.

THE WRESTLING MATCH

CHAPTER 1

MY FAMILY

I LOVED MY FAMILY. They loved me. I loved my mother, my father, my brother and my three sisters.

I was born into a comfortable San Francisco family. My dad, the Assistant District Attorney under Matt Brady, was a smart, well known and respected lawyer. A devout Catholic, he ushered every Sunday morning at the 6:30 Mass. He lived his religion at home, in his professional life and in volunteer work for The City's street people.

My mother had been the District Attorney's secretary. That's how Mother and Daddy met. We always called him "Daddy", because that's what my mother always called him – Daddy Dear. It was a nice name, especially when there was a young child in the house. And there was a child for many years. Five of us, spread out over a twelve year age difference. Toots (Dorothy) the oldest, Terry (Theresa), Harmon (and that's what we called him), Joe (Joseph, *me*) and my baby sister Ronni (Veronica).

Typical of the times, Mother stayed home and was the daily influence on all of us. Daddy left early, took the streetcar downtown to work, then back home in the evening. While the norm was that we kids ate dinner early, often enough we'd wait until my dad got home. Then it was a full-family meal. Mother was constantly present to us. Daddy's presence was routinely just in the evenings, Monday through Friday.

Mother was the rudder that kept the family and each of us individually going straight ahead. She's the one who talked to the teachers when necessary, took us to the doctor when necessary, helped us with our homework when necessary, broke up the fights when necessary and apologized to the neighbors when necessary. She loved us and we knew it. She was the visible giver, helper, encourager. She was Mother.

My dad usually seemed serious, especially around us children. Not aloof, but solemn. When I got older, I became aware that he had a significant fun side. He loved to take Mother to a party and every now and then hosted one at home.

When we had company, there would be plenty of laughter, as there was, so I'm told, when he was out with his friends. But at home, my dad usually was pretty straight. Every night, whether he got home early or late, he'd ask us about school. Early on, I may not have comprehended the concept of "priority", but it became clear that our schooling was important to him and he expected us to do well. Very well.

Three girls. My oldest sister, Toots, was brilliant. She didn't just get all A's. Her grades were all A+. She was very warm, nurturing, kind. She was everything you can imagine in a terrific older sister. My favorite sibling. We had a close relationship. To me, she stood apart from the other siblings in that she showed me a lot of attention and affection. She always had a smile and a hug for me. I felt special when I was with her. Special. This relationship was an early influence on my self-confidence. Because of her constant attention, kindness and encouragement, I could feel good about myself, trust myself and like myself. As much as anyone, my Big Sister wrote a lot of positive messages onto my *tabula rasa*, that blank page.

Terry, the second child, was often sick, so not too cheery. She was also the bossy one, so I didn't enjoy her very much. Always critical, she delighted in telling me what I was doing wrong, how I was not measuring up, how I needed to improve. So while Toots was regularly encouraging me with positive, self-confident messages, Terry was sending self-doubt messages constantly. That produced the daily wrestling match between self-doubt and self-confidence that I mentioned earlier. I both liked myself and doubted myself. Terry, however, like all people, did have her bright star. She is the one who took care of Mother when she became stricken with Alzheimer's.

Veronica was my baby sister. When we both were of grade school age, I became her self-appointed guardian, walking her back and forth to school. I don't remember that much about her before she was six or seven. When she became school age, however, I felt a sense of importance taking care of her. Was this a form of confidence? Yes, but it was not self-confidence. It was what-I-can-do confidence, achievement confidence, skill confidence. All good and important, but not **self**-confidence. (I'll explain the difference later in Chapter 22.)

My older brother, Harmon. The #1 boy. Like Toots, he was a brain. Pulled straight "A's" all through eight grades of grammar school. We got along quite well. Being just 13 months apart, we'd fight, but we'd also laugh together, play together, walk to school together and get in trouble together. At one point in our young lives we became known in the family as The Buster and The Breaker. Always, however, there was that haunting feeling that he was better than I. He was smarter and constantly praised for this. I couldn't get rid of that feeling of jealousy. Unable to identify it or understand it at the time, I made it more about me than him and turned it into self-doubt. I was behind him on the calendar, behind him in brains, behind him in parental praise. I wasn't as good. Comparison and jealousy led to self-doubt.

This jealousy deeply influenced my life. I carried it with me until he died. I was jealous of his intelligence and his consequent successes. I let that jealousy lead me to doubt myself, think I am not enough, think I don't belong. Our relationship seemed normal to most people, but to me it was burdened by this comparison I clung to. As life continued, we spoke regularly – family get togethers, occasionally water skiing or playing golf together. Few of our conversations were deep and personal. For sure I never told him that I was jealous of him.

Strangely, I found out after he died that he was always jealous of me! I was shocked. I compared myself to him and ranked myself less than him all my life. Self-doubt. He compared himself to me and ranked himself less than me. Unknowingly, regrettably, both of us fed our self-doubt at the expense of each other. How sad.

The ultimate evil of jealousy is not that my brother or my mom or dad told me I was not as good as my brother. It was that I was telling myself that I was not as good as him. All self-doubt; no self-confidence.

CHAPTER 2

THE DOG HOUSE

I DON'T REMEMBER HAVING a feeling of competition with any of my sisters. But it was there with my brother. And strong!

From when I can remember, he was better than I. Always over-weight, always a little chunky, I felt less attractive compared to him. He was slender, the way a boy should be. His hair was black, shiny and always neat. Mine was dull brown and haphazard. He was handsome. I was puffy enough that they called me "Apple Cheeks". While most days we just got along, there were moments when these differences bothered me consciously.

The biggest difference was the brains. Straight "A's" for him. I'd be thrilled if I got a "B". Mostly "C's" for me, only rarely an A. As my dad emphasized the importance of school and grades, I felt even more *secondary* to my brother. I couldn't keep up with him. I couldn't compete.

I admit that he was a good brother. We played together, went to school together, did homework together, got along pretty well for the most part. Together we'd drive our parents crazy, get into all kinds of mischief and stand up for each other if we were in real trouble. The problem wasn't my brother. It wasn't his fault that he was super smart, wasn't his fault that he was better looking, wasn't his fault that he was older. The problem was mine, that combination of my own jealousy and self-doubt that robbed me of self-confidence at an early age.

At the time, I would not have used the terms self-doubt and self-confidence. But looking back, these two labels described something real in my inner being, my core, my soul. Feelings of self-doubt were much stronger than self-confidence.

This incident I do recall vividly. We had company for dinner. We kids ate early, then to our rooms to do our homework. As he did often, my dad called us to the living room to tell the guest couple about our day at school. (Ronni was not in school yet, so she was excused.) Toots made her little presentation. Excellent. Applause. Terry did the same, a little more hesitant but still drawing applause. Then Harmon. He was really good. Big applause. Joe's turn. Feeling embarrassed, I stumbled through my recall of the day. When I finished, my mother and father together blurted, "Very good, Dear". But no one clapped. No applause. Self-doubt.

Looking back, I know my parents liked me and loved me very much, but I became blinded by these comparisons to my brother. I perceived these experiences as a subtle statement that I was not as good, not good enough, not enough. Self-doubt.

(Little did I know at the time, but this practice of my dad making us tell company about our day in school was a blessing for me. That early experience played an important part in getting me to the point where I could say, "Finally, I like myself.")

At some point it became obvious that I was not going to win my parents' attention and approval because of brains, because of my school work. No matter how important it was to my dad that I excel in school, I knew it wasn't going to happen. I had to find another way to make them proud of me, another vehicle for attracting their admiration, my own reason for liking myself.

I took to fixing things.

Without being told, I cleaned up the ugly oil drip spot on the garage floor. "Oh, that looks good; good job," my dad commented when he got home. I straightened up the huge firewood box in the basement. "Oh, that's great," my dad commented. I fixed a broken trellis behind Mother's favorite rose bush. "Oh, thank you, dear. That's so thoughtful of you." I repaired a huge crack in the back yard concrete slab. "You're a big help," encouraged my dad. These were whole new experiences– regular acknowledgement of jobs well done.

After these little, tentative steps into my self-created realm of importance, one day I decided to undertake a major project. "Daddy," I announced, "Wolf needs a new doghouse. Can we go to the hardware store Saturday and buy the wood?" He said, "Yes."

So that Saturday morning the two of us got in the car and drove to the hardware store. I felt so special. It was just Daddy and me. No one else, especially not my very smart brother. The owner welcomed us. My dad, hand on my shoulder, said, "Ralph, this is my son Joseph. He wants to build a doghouse." I remember feeling excited. But even more, I felt proud standing there, being introduced by my dad. This was special. I felt good about myself. At the moment, I was very comfortable being me.

We bought everything we needed for a simple doghouse. Even a can of paint to protect it from the San Francisco fog. Over the next few weeks, my dad guided me and helped me. He taught me how to make a basic drawing, how to measure accurately, how to saw, hammer and nail. Patiently he stayed with me, showing me what to do, but letting me do it. This was going to be my project that he helped me with; not his project that I helped him with! The final step was painting Wolf's name over the entrance in bright red letters. After it was finished, my dad asked Mother to take our picture – me, holding Wolf in my arms in front of the house and Daddy, proudly wrapping his big arm around my shoulders. I was witnessing confidence, self-confidence. Not because of the dog house I built, but because of my dad standing next to me with his arm proudly, lovingly and encouragingly around my shoulder. For this moment, I was very happy being me.

My brother wasn't there. He was probably up in our room studying.

I was still pudgy, still not as smart as my brother, but I built a doghouse and everybody loved it. Toots, Terry, Harmon, Ronni, Mother and Daddy. Everybody. Even the dog!

I felt I had found my niche, my special place in the family, a reason for my mom and dad to see me as special. A reason for *myself* to see me as special. Looking back, this was probably the first major step I took in the gradual process of moving from self-doubt to self-confidence.

I was Joe, The Fixer. Finally, I knew my dad was proud of me. And I was proud of myself.

CHAPTER 3

MY DAD'S CONTINUED INFLUENCE

CULTURALLY AND ECONOMICALLY IDENTIFIED in what was known as the upper middle class, my parents were generous in providing our material needs and most of our wants.....plenty of toys, always well dressed, fun summer vacations at Hoberg's, the Russian River or a trip to one of the National Parks. They sent all five of us to Catholic school, a costly undertaking.

More important than the fine material environment was the spiritual life they taught us. Once my dad completed his task as an usher at the 6:30 Mass, he'd drive home, pick us all up and drive the whole family to the 9 o'clock Mass. God and family were important to both my parents.

Unappreciated at the time, while I was struggling with my brother's presumed superiority, Mother and Daddy – especially my dad – were sowing seeds of self-confidence. When I built that dog house for Wolf, my dad did not just help me, he encouraged me, taught me, guided me and, in the end, praised me. Those were unforgettable lessons. They were seeds of self-confidence. Merely seeds, dormant in my soul. But they were there, alive, waiting to sprout.

My dad was not athletic, but he enjoyed walking. Often I'd go with him, pulling Wolf on a short lead. One afternoon we were up by the reservoir, able to see clearly the Golden Gate Bridge. I, The Fixer, remember thinking that it was beautiful, but too massive and too complicated a structure. I commented aloud, "I could never build anything like that!" He immediately countered, "Sure you could. All you'd have to do is get whatever help you need. Then you could build it." No doubt, simply obvious to him. He announced this as such a matter of fact that I'm sure it burned into my soul. I don't know if I believed it at the time, but I remember the incident, where we were standing, the view of The City's Sunset District homes, the stately bridge in the distance. I remembered it years later. Eventually it became part of my thinking, part of my belief system. It was another one of those seeds that eventually would become a strong source of self-confidence. I could build the Golden Gate Bridge.

Writing and public speaking were important to my dad – key skills in his legal profession. He first helped me with writing, patiently showing me how to improve what I had written. He kept telling me that people would always enjoy an interesting, well written story. And, incidentally, they would always listen to a good speech. The more often I wrote, the more often he would say, "That's good." Another seed coming to bloom. I was beginning to understand confidence, feel it, each time he said, "That's good."

All throughout grammar school, he continued that practice of having us tell company about our day at school. I gradually noticed I was becoming more and more comfortable and confident each time I had to 'perform". Daddy encouraged: stand up straight; enunciate; look at us; stop saying "uuh". Probably I didn't speak as well as Toots or Harmon, but I could sense growing approval from my dad. Together with my mom and their guests, he would clap and say, "Very good."

While I still felt like #2 to my brother, I was beginning to realize that there was talent, value and worth in this particular #2 by the name of Joseph Skillin. Self-doubt was slowly, ever so slowly, giving way to the beginnings of self-confidence.

MOTHER'S UNINTENTIONAL MISTAKE

THERE WAS NEVER ANY question about my mother's love for me or any of us. She had a warm heart, an even-keeled disposition and an ever-present desire to encourage us. One way or another, the message she expressed was, "Whatever you are, be the best."

All five of us kids heard that almost daily, whether walking out to go to school, sitting at the breakfast table or dining room table, or in our rooms doing our homework. It was a message deeply carved onto that *tabula rasa*. This encouragement came from pure love. All she wanted was the best for us, back then at school and later through our entire lives.

An easy generator of self-doubt is comparison. When I compared myself to my brother, I stirred up self-doubt. When I compared myself to my middle sister's unmet standards, I generated more self-doubt. When I compared myself to neighbors

Billy, Red and Tommy, all more athletic than I, I deepened my self-doubt.

But there could be no more strong and terrible cause of self-doubt than my mother demanding that I **be the best!** That is a call to be better than everyone in all things. In fact impossible, but that was hardly the problem. It is a call to judge everyone and see their level of success. It is a call to measure my own level of success against everyone else's. It is a call for me to compare always, see myself as falling short and increasing my self-doubt. How could I be the best without measuring myself against everyone?

Much better if she had advised, "Do *your* best. Be *your* best." These still would have encouraged us to be well and do well. Acknowledging young imperfection, need for development and wisdom, the challenge to be one's best eliminates the need to compare self to anyone else and everyone else. With no comparisons, no jealousy, no feeling of not belonging, there would be so much less self-doubt.

Apart from challenging – almost demanding – us to compare ourselves to everyone so we could become the best, Mother inadvertently challenged the five of us to compare ourselves to each other. The self-doubt vs self-confidence wrestling match was going strong. In my personal match, self-doubt was winning.

CHAPTER 5

POINTS TO REMEMBER #1

I WANT TO PAUSE the telling of my life story in order to point out some important truths.

1. We are born with a *tabula rasa*. We are not born with self-doubt. Nor do I think we are born with self-confidence. In our youngest years, other people influence us with their words and actions. Obviously, parents have the greatest influence on us. When they use negative, hostile, derogatory or insulting words in speaking to us and about us, they are planting the seeds of self-doubt. Warm, loving, supportive words and actions build self-confidence.

2. Before school age, our feelings of confidence and doubt are influenced heavily by siblings. A common danger is that in comparing ourselves to our siblings, we can easily find room to doubt ourselves. Conversely, a loving, nurturing sibling can strongly influence our self-confidence.

3. Early-child playmates who are more skilled than we, feed our self-doubt.

4. Jealousy is poison to self-confidence. It is a comparison that I use to brand myself as less good, less able, less important.

5. Childhood successes (skills, and desired accomplishments) support and strengthen our confidence in self.

6. When we reach high school age, generally we are more self-conscience. Most people become more self-judging and self-doubting at this age.

7. If we are willing to take some risks, we can build some measure of confidence through achievements and successes.

8. Achievement-confidence is different than self-confidence.

9. The wrestling match between self-doubt and self-confidence continues throughout our life.

CHASING SELF-CONFIDENCE

• C H A P T E R   6 •

BOARDING SCHOOL

AFTER GRADUATING FROM THE Eighth Grade, I followed my brother to a boarding school for my high school education. Actually it was the seminary, where young men started their training to become Catholic priests. At this young age, going to the seminary was not really my personal choice. Encouragement from my family and the teachers in my catholic grammar school set a course that I followed without much thought. "You'd make a good priest," they repeated. "You're going to go to the seminary", they repeated. And so I did.

I wasn't alone there, since my brother was in the same school. Yet living in a semi-monastic atmosphere of silence and separation, I felt pretty much alone most of the time. In those days, when a seminary typically emphasized quiet and solitude, it was natural to feel quiet, apart and alone. Fitting in would have been difficult for me in any circumstances, but with my major case of self-doubt, it was even harder. I wasn't a complete hermit, but the opportunity for making friends was minimal. At least for me, the self-doubter. I was shy, timid and uncomfortable around strangers. Do I fit in here? Will I be accepted? Will these students like me? I just felt so uncomfortable with all these strangers, new classmates. The small beginnings of self-confidence that sprung up in the seventh and eighth grade would now be challenged by the heavy self-doubting in this totally new environment.

I enjoyed my school work there. Fortunately we had small classes, taught by teachers who worked hard at helping us learn. Academically it was a good environment for me. Whereas back home, in grammar school, I struggled to get B's, here I did much better. This part of my life was positive. In the end, I graduated with honors. Class work was the one area that provided some basis for what I believed was self-confidence. But it was not self-confidence. Rather it was a new sense of confidence in my scholastic abilities, achievement-confidence that I can do well in school.

Any feeling of confidence garnered through my studies and class work was diminished by self-doubt in the social aspect of school life. I wasn't weird or deliberately anti-social, but clearly I was not a joiner. I hated standing around in a group of fellow students. I always felt I had nothing to add to the conversation. I was reluctant to join any of the sports teams, because I wasn't good at baseball, basketball or track. I didn't fit. I couldn't compete. I would not be welcomed.

This self-doubt, this aloneness, this reluctance I could not blame on my brother or my family. It was just me. What may have begun with jealousy toward my brother I recognized now as my own self-doubt. Introspectively doubting, judging myself to not fit in socially, I struggled with confidence. Because I did well in school, because I was able to develop fairly decent relationships with two or three "pretty good" friends, I was still OK. I wasn't miserable, not a recluse, didn't cry myself to sleep at night. I was OK. With just enough early onset confidence to get me by. And enough confidence to want more.

More self-confidence. That's what I wanted. But how would I ever get it?

Remember Wolf's dog house? Remember the rewards of praise? Remember how I felt a newfound surge of confidence? Well, if it worked then, it might work again.

Bring back The Fixer.

CHAPTER 7

FINDING MY PLACE

"BEFORE WE CAN BECOME self-confident, we need to have the courage to accept that we are who we are." *(author unknown)* When I entered the seminary, I was The Fixer in the Skillin household. I was proud of that and was comfortable accepting that as a definition of me.

My new school had two large sports fields, with only one person, Bill, to care for them. This was my opportunity. The Fixer. Instead of standing around uncomfortably in my free time, I could contribute to something worthwhile. Instead of standing aside, aloof, I could step up, get involved. Instead of wasting life in self-doubt, I could get active and find some confidence. I am The Fixer, I realized. So with confidence I offered to help Bill.

But self-doubt jumped to the front of the line when I first talked to Bill. *Great, he said. I'd love to have the help. Do you know how to run a tractor?*

No. (Get real. I'm a city boy. We don't have tractors in San Francisco.)

Do you know how to lay out a football field versus a soccer field?

No. (Aren't they pretty much the same?)

Could you.... Could you.... Could you....?

No. No. No.

That's OK, he said. I'll teach you as we go along. I'm just happy to have the help.

Fortunately, Bill was desperate for help. The fact that he would teach me everything raised my spirits and gave me hope. Excited, I just stayed with him that afternoon, helping him measure and chalk the football field (as opposed to a soccer field!) The Fixer.

Bill and I became known as "the campus crew". The more I worked with him, the more I learned. The more I learned, the more I wanted to do. I learned how to run that tractor, even how to repair it. I learned how to lay out a field – football, soccer or baseball. We even built a small cabin where students could go when it rained – to smoke or play cards or just sit around a fire.

The most important thing I learned about was myself. I was beginning to understand who I was, what made me tick. I was a person that had something to offer. It wasn't just a talent or a skill. It was me, myself. Fixing things was simply *an expression* of me, but it was *I* who was at the core of it. I had value. I counted. I belonged. Here there was no need for my brother, no comparison to him. Here there was no need for my scolding middle sister. Here was just me in my own new environment. I could just be me. I was comfortable being me.

As I was getting more and more comfortable, the self-doubt was diminishing and the self-confidence was expanding in my mind, my heart and my soul. I was learning to trust myself.

CHAPTER 8

ACHIEVEMENTS AND SUCCESSES

W HEN I WAS ABOUT 4, I learned to swim. Sort of. It was more splashing while somehow staying afloat than it was anything else. But it was fun. We would all swim during our family vacations. Throughout the year, my brother and I would go swim at the YMI every Saturday morning.

In my first two years of high school, I was still an awkward, splashy swimmer. In my junior year the school offered swimming lessons by a professional swimming coach. At first reluctant to sign up because I knew I could swim, a friend convinced me to go for lessons anyway. What a change! The coach taught me to really swim, not just stay afloat while thrashing around in the water. The new style was less strenuous and more fun. The more sleek style, compared to the previous jerking-windmill style, made me imagine I was a dolphin, smoothly gliding through my natural habitat. Suddenly swimming was more than just exercising or having fun in the water. It became a relaxing, quiet escape into a new world of peaceful solitude. I was alone, but enjoying the solitude. I was comfortable here. I felt I belonged here. I swam more and more, getting better and better.

In my senior year of high school I was asked to be on the varsity swim team. How exciting! And what a boost to my confidence. I was on swim teams throughout my college years, excelling in freestyle and the back stroke, winning medals, building my confidence.

Another sport skill that seemed to build my confidence was soccer. I did not have the skills needed for baseball or basketball. Nor did I have the finesse to play the type of soccer that one would call "the beautiful sport". There was nothing beautiful about the way we played soccer. We looked and acted more like a group of defensive backs from Oklahoma.

In this environment I was good, accepted as one of the better players. I was agile enough, fast enough and heavy enough to be good. Being heavy allowed me to bump opponents aside, knock them down if necessary, move the ball downfield or keep an opponent away from our goal. I became very good at this. It built my ego. It added to my confidence.

The Fixer was broadening his image. Add The Swimmer and The Soccer Player.

Recall, however, Henri Nouwen's quote. "Original sin is man's endless capacity for self-rejection." With all the good in my life, with the new skills, successes and acceptance, self-doubt re-established this form of original sin within me. While I was moving ahead with my own life, my own identity, my capacity to define and accept who I was, comparisons to my brother clawed at me. I just seemed unable to get rid of them. He was still smarter than I. He was doing better academically than I. Even giving myself credit for tracking toward a *magna cum laude*, he was tracking toward a *summa cum laude*. Those brains of his! The brains my dad appreciated and honored. Where it mattered most (I still believed, though erroneously) I was still #2. Exactly where I started.

Self-doubt is like a vulture. Swat it away and it soon comes back to claim its prey. All these new and consistent achievements and successes were not strong enough to keep the vulture away.

• C H A P T E R   9 •

SKILLS FOR LIFE

W HILE SWIMMING AND SOCCER were fun, they would not be a way to make a living – at least not for me. I needed to develop other skills that would serve me well as an adult, especially as a priest. Skills and confidence are not the same thing, but for me (and I suspect for you) finding, developing and honing skills is a sure path to some degree of confidence.

Away at the seminary for high school, then four more years of college and another four years of post-grad studies, I developed two specific skills in which I take a measure of pride: writing and public speaking. Even if pride is not warranted, I thoroughly enjoy these skills.

It was my dad who first encouraged me to write – urging me, correcting me, helping me. Since it was one of his skills, he knew how to start me in that same direction. He began back when I was in the sixth or seventh grade. A time when I still succumbed to self-doubt, it gave me an initial spark of confidence – not just because I was improving a new skill but because I was being taught by my dad. Special attention. Improvement. Praise. Recognition. The beginnings of self-confidence.

In high school, I started writing for the school paper, just as Daddy had done at his school. I selected the stories I wanted to write, edited and re-edited them before submission, made my deadlines and usually got positive feedback. All this was good for me in building confidence. It also gave me a skill that would be important and useful throughout my life. Most importantly, however, it was folding back the curtains on Joe Skillin, revealing more of who I am. No longer was I just The Fixer, The Swimmer and The Soccer Player. I was also The Writer. And, unable to write well without some degree of intelligence, I was beginning to realize that I was smart. And it didn't even occur to me to ask if I were as smart as my brother. I didn't care. It didn't matter. I realized I was smart. That's all that mattered.

I was liking myself more, becoming more comfortable with myself, trusting myself more. While I still experienced self-doubts, confidence was strengthening. While most of this new confidence was in new skills, what I was achieving, I sensed that *self*-confidence was flourishing also.

The second life skill I developed in school was public speaking. With the help of excellent teachers, I became good at it, quickly grew into it, became so comfortable with it. Even today, if someone were to ask me what skill is my personal favorite, I would answer: public speaking. Any talk I give, to a business group, at church or a social gathering, I approach with the utmost confidence. Of course, every good talk takes preparation – knowing your audience, picking an appropriate topic, gathering and organizing pertinent information, practice. It also takes skilled presentation – eye contact, articulation, rhythm. Since I work on each of these elements before any presentation, I am confident and comfortable standing before an audience.

Public speaking gave me early insights into what real self-confidence is. Yes, speaking nourished achievement-confidence in me, but I could tell there was more, something different, something intangible, something that touched my very soul. When I spoke, it was not just words, not just a message, not a performance. I was not just confident about my preparation and presentation, content and delivery. I was confident about me. Not just confident about the talk, but about the speaker, me.

When I entered St. Joseph school, I had little self-confidence and an abundance of self-doubt. I possessed only the young seeds of self-confidence, planted by my loving family, especially my dad. In school, along with the development of several skills, I made significant growth in confidence.

It is significant that I developed these skills without reference to my brother. They were my achievements, without any comparison to whatever he was doing with his life.. There was a purity in my goals, the work to achieve them and the success of achieving them.. I didn't need to rank myself against Harmon. These were my goals, my achievements, pure and simple. And I liked myself for achieving them, trusted myself as being able, worthy, capable. I was comfortable being the unique and special person that accomplished all this. I was self-confident.

At least I thought I was.

FATHER JOE

I WAS ORDAINED A Catholic priest in 1961 in Oakland, California. I was popular as a young parish priest in my first assignment. I worked hard at my priestly duties and became immediately known for my hope-filled sermons. I regularly administered to the many elderly people in convalescent homes and almost daily tried to comfort those dying or near death in Kaiser Emergency. Always with a smile, I set up a teen club and shepherded the many kids in the parish. I was doing well, accepted and popular. Not bragging. I mention these facts so I can make an important point later.

Just one year after ordination I was assigned to be secretary and vice-chancellor of the diocese. That was an honor, but it also entailed more office work than among-the-people work. Preferring the latter, I busied myself with teaching a religion class at the Catholic high school. I sought out and was appointed a member of the Social Justice Committee. The Mayor of Oakland appointed me a member of the Oakland Housing Authority. I hosted a weekly TV show on Oakland's Channel 2. I was appointed Director of Public Relations for the Diocese of Oakland. I was doing well, accepted and popular.

Except for the Social Justice appointment, I did not seek any of these connections. They just seemed to come to me, one after the other. As I fell into these new roles, I felt more and more comfortable, sure of myself. It was a time of my life when I lived without jealousy over my brother or judgments from my sister. I was just being myself, growing, expanding, gaining confidence. I was just happy being uniquely myself.

Eventually I was appointed pastor of the cathedral, located across the street from Oakland's Greyhound Depot. This was a challenging but delightful and wonderful conglomeration of every ethnic, social, religious and cultural subset of humanity. To serve them all, I put priority energy into Sunday Mass and its preparation. On a normal Sunday, we would gather about 1800 people attending two Masses. Weekdays were filled with a variety of meetings, services, ministries, discussions and visits with my downtown neighbors. I was doing well, accepted and popular.

Joe, The Fixer, The Writer and The Speaker was now Father Joe – fixer of souls, writer of religious articles, speaker of TV interviews and sermons. Doing very well, both popular and accepted. I loved what I was doing.

But I still lived with ever-present self-doubt. Self-confidence did not match performance. I have pointed out all my accomplishments not to brag, but to make this important point which I cannot stress enough: there is a distinction between self-confidence and popularity, between self-confidence and acceptance by others, between self-confidence and accomplishment. Despite all those successes, I was not genuinely self-confident.

I wrote earlier, "I loved what I was doing." The key word is "doing". What I was doing was good, helpful to others. I felt good about what I was doing, sure that it was helping people. But to me, to my core, to my soul, it was all external. I judged it to be all out there, not deeply within me, not part of my soul, my inner being.

The wrestling match between self-doubt and self-confidence continued. As there were real signs indicating self-confidence, so there were many signs indicating my lack of confidence These were secret signs, known to me alone. I could disguise and hide them from others. While everyone judged the Father Joe I allowed them to see, everyone thought I was an extremely confident man. But what I did not allow my parishioners to see was the self-doubting Father Joe.

When I entered the church for the 10 o'clock Mass, the most popular one, I always walked up the side aisle to get to the sacristy. I felt uneasy about walking up the main aisle with so many early attendees already in the pews. I worried they would be judging me, my work, my daily life. Judging my sermons, my ministry to the poor, even judging the way I walked, the way I let my hair grow. Comparing. Comparing to what? It wasn't the parishioners that were comparing and judging. I was the one comparing and judging. I was comparing myself, the real me, to a fictitious *ME* and worried that I wasn't as good as I should be, could be. Self-doubt.

When Mass was over, I stood outside the main doors to greet people, much like all ministers on any Sunday morning. I was truly uncomfortable doing this. Again, self-doubt made me wonder what they thought of my sermon. I stood there with I'm-not-good-enough conviction, looking for an excuse to break away, go back to the sacristy to change out of my liturgical vestments and return to the quiet of the rectory. I was comfortable with friends but still so self-doubting with strangers.

I officiated at hundreds of weddings. Both because I was invited and because I wanted to honor the bride and groom, I would attend the reception whenever possible. I was always welcomed. As I walked toward the reception line, people would comment on how nice the ceremony was. I'd smile, say a thank you and move on. I wasn't cold or rude. I just didn't linger, because I was uncomfortable. After greeting the bride, groom and their families, usually I would immediately leave. If someone tried to get me to stay, I'd respond, "Thanks, but I really have to get back." For a busy priest, it was an accepted excuse which also hid my combination of discomfort, self-doubt and lack of confidence in myself. Popularity is not self-confidence. Neither is achievement.

Being a priest was such a wonderful part of my life. I was truly blessed. I enjoyed it humanly, religiously, culturally, spiritually. In some ways, the best part of it was being able to help people heal on a daily basis. Constantly, people, hurting, came to me for help. I listened well and most often was able to offer some degree of help. Still and always, The Fixer.

As a little child, I was dying to get more attention. Here, in my thirties, I was getting more attention than most people get in a lifetime. But all the attention and the developed skills and the popularity could not give me the self-confidence I had missed since childhood. I was still having trouble liking myself, liking my *Self.*

CHAPTER 11

POINTS TO REMEMBER #2

1. Develop your talents. They encourage you to move toward self-confidence.

2. There is a distinction between self-confidence and popularity

3. .... between self-confidence and acceptance by others

4. .... between self-confidence and excellent work.

5. Excellent work, acceptance and popularity are external.

6. Self-confidence is internal.

7. The wrestling match between self-doubt and self-confidence continues throughout our lives.

DISCOVERING AFFIRMATIONS

THE OMEGA SEMINAR

THE OMEGA SEMINAR WAS one of California's ubiquitous self-help, deep-growth, multi-day workshops designed to make anyone a more successful person. A few friends who had attended this particular seminar suggested I go to it. I got the literature, read it carefully and found some immediate interest. I asked my friends to tell me more. The more I heard, the more I was interested. This was not one of those crazy seminars where you ate money, smoked pot, sat around in hot tubs overlooking the Pacific and meditated to the soothing feel of ostrich feathers being dragged gently across your body. No, Omega was three days of lectures, study, Q&A and an impressive workbook. Not play, but hard, serious work. One friend even told me, "Father Joe, you could even use some of this stuff in your sermons." I signed up.

What caught my attention in the literature was that the seminar's main purpose was to help people become more self-confident. One of the main tenants of the seminar was based on the affirmation *I Like Myself*. Obviously this got my interest. As I read further, I understood the emphasis on accepting oneself as fundamentally worthy, embracing oneself as is, being comfortable with oneself and trusting oneself. I wasn't sure how all this could be accomplished in just three days, but I was more than willing to go find out. I decided to attend.

Most people that attended the Omega seminar were business executives whose primary goal was to improve their company's success. Advertised additional goals were reducing stress, getting along better with their spouses, becoming better golfers and improving health. In short, attendees could improve any aspect of their lives they wanted. Those promises were the statement of Omega's marketing team, listing enticing benefits to the general public. Actually, Omega delivered on these promises. There were separate sessions on income, health, relationships and more, each providing tools that could be personalized and used for an individual's increasing success.

The founder and our teacher, John Boyle, saw these benefits as secondary. What was most important to him was that his students first become more confident people. He generalized, "Without strong confidence, without believing in yourself, you will always run into limitations in achieving your goals, in chasing your desires for and definitions of successes." Therefore, rather than starting the three-day seminar with strategies to improve wealth, skills and relationships, Mr. Boyle started with Maxwell Maltz's belief that most people achieve around only 20% of their potential. We are severely limited, he explained, at our earliest age by parents sending normal messages such as "You can't do that" or "Keep your mouth shut" or "That's all right dear; if college is too hard, you can always get a job at

Macy's." Another sneakily negative message he mentioned was my mother's words: "Whatever you do, be the best." Denials, comparisons, limitations, presumptions of inability – specific or implied. Mr. Boyle explained that these early negative, limiting messages reside in our subconscious mind forever, like a recorded tape that replays unceasingly. Molding our self-image, they affect our decisions, our feelings about ourselves and our levels of achievement. They do their negative work even if we are not aware of them.

We can overcome those old negative beliefs, Mr. Boyle contended, by countering them with opposite, positive statements (affirmations) repeating them so often that they overwhelm the original negative statements. For example, sufficiently repeating "I like myself" will eventually overcome the memory of your dad often having said to you as a child, "Why can't you be good, like your sister?" (This is one example, mentioned out of context and full explanation, but it gives a sense of Boyle's teaching.) He contends that from our earliest days we have been programmed through others' words and actions to be limited, to be thus and so, to achieve in this area, to feel inadequate in this arena, to be comfortable here, self-doubting there. But we can change most of the negative influence through affirmations. We can change what we were taught about ourselves years ago. We can rewrite the *tabula rasa*. We can change **ourselves.**

When I was in school, I studied philosophy for six years. I enjoyed learning about how so many people interpret life and living, how people try to understand the human condition, how we become who we are, achieve what we do and yet fail so miserably in other areas. Given this personal background and preparation, I was so comfortable with Mr. Boyle, his teaching and his seminar that the day I returned home I started doing affirmations.

It just so happened that every man and woman who attended Omega with me was a business executive – CEO, CFO, Vice-president. There was a cocktail party the final evening during which we were encouraged to talk about out three-day experience. I noted that the great majority were motivated to work harder and smarter at their business, improve some personal skill or heal a wounded relationship. All admirable goals. But goals they were, external achievements, all about *doing* better. Yes, they were all motivated by the Omega Seminar.

But I was inspired by it.

I became convinced that I could overpower my many forms of self-doubt, decrease all the negative comparisons that I thought of daily, stop most of those useless, arbitrary negative judgements about myself, even rid myself of the life-long jealousy I harbored against my brother.

I was inspired to improve my self-confidence, make it the foundation of my normal daily attitude. And the tool to accomplish all this was so simple. Affirmations. I realized that these changes would not just happen automatically. I'd have to make them happen. I'd have to put in the work. But I was inspired. Therefore I was willing to put in the work.

I have been doing affirmations virtually every day for fifty years. They have been key in helping me move from self-doubt to self-confidence. They have enabled self-confidence to win that wrestling match 90% of the time. They have helped me move toward honestly accepting who I am, being fully comfortable with myself, honestly trusting myself. The very definition of self-confidence.

CHAPTER 13

WHAT IS AN AFFIRMATION?

THE SINGLE, SIMPLE EXERCISE that Mr. Boyle used for improving our lives was the affirmation. It is important, therefore, to understand affirmations if you want to improve your self-confidence, as I did. I'll write much more about affirmations later in this book.

A classic affirmation is a positive statement about oneself or about another. A good teacher might affirm a student by saying, "You are really good at math, Billy." Or I might affirm myself by explicitly thinking (internally saying) "I'm a really good golfer."

However, an affirmation in the sense Boyle used it can be negative. "You'll never be good at math, Billy. Try social studies." Or, "Oh, I always mess up my talks." Positive affirmations can build our self-confidence. Negative affirmations build our self-doubt.

The Omega Seminar taught students how to succeed in two areas: personal acceptance and skill improvement -- improvement in business, home life, relationships, sports, virtue. To the extent we hold positive thoughts about self, we move towards self-acceptance and personal growth. An affirmation, such as "I like myself" can build one's self-confidence over time. To the extent we harbor negative thoughts about any particular skill or virtue, we hold ourselves back. For example, if I keep thinking as I'm driving to the golf course – and when I'm actually playing a round – that I'm not particularly good at golf, I'm not going to get much better, no matter how hard I try. I don't even need to say the words aloud. All I have to do is think them!

This book is not a treatise on affirmations. But to help you understand them a little better, here are a few more quick examples. An affirmation is a mental tool that helps you move from where you are to where you want to be. If I am fairly impatient, repeating the affirmation "I am patient in all situations" will lead me to a greater degree of patience. Constantly affirming "I enjoy and am successful at math" will lead me toward succeeding at math. If my oldest child regularly gets on my nerves, the helpful affirmation is, "I have special warm regards for Billy." If I'm always a nervous wreck, I would affirm, "I easily relax, as deeply as I wish, at any time." Prioritizing the day for the always-hassled manager can become de-stressed by, "I do everything right now as it needs doing." Affirmations presume an ongoing problem that you want to overcome – an attitude (e.g., anger), a habit (e.g., nail biting), a vice (e.g., excessive drinking) or simply a sub-par performance (e.g., golf) that you wish to improve. They look to the future, to what you want to become, how you want to be.

My self-thought rules. Even if I hang on to those old negative thoughts programed into my *tabula rasa* twenty, thirty or forty years ago, they strongly influence my level of achievement. This is true in business, in all sports, in study and learning skills, in family relations and in individual, personal growth. So if self-thought rules, the key is to have positive self-thoughts. A positive affirmation (self-thought statement), repeated again and again and again, eventually overwhelms and replaces a negative self-thought. Retrain your mind and you eventually change your beliefs and behavior.

I LIKE MYSELF UNCONDITIONALLY.

I AM REALLY COMFORTABLE BEING THE UNIQUE AND VERY SPECIAL PERSON THAT I AM.

There were other affirmations, but these two changed my life. Truly I was inspired. I started repeating them, every morning and every evening. I have continued to do this every day for 50 years. They are only mental tools but they have enabled me over time to start accepting who I am and grow in self-confidence. "I'm not just The Fixer or The Swimmer or The Speaker. I'm Joseph Skillin and I become more and more confident in being me." I was growing in self-confidence.

When I first started doing affirmations, that wrestling match of doubt vs confidence was still present, but quickly self-confidence became stronger. Not a clear winner, but clearly stronger. Soon I had enough self-confidence to struggle through a seismic change in my life.

CHAPTER 14

A MAJOR LIFE CHANGE

About two years after I attended the Omega Seminar, I decided to confront and answer the biggest question of my entire life. This was an enormous struggle. Simply explained, I wanted to get married but I did not want to leave the priesthood. For several years I had conducted couples' weekend retreats at Clear Lake. There were times when it seemed to me that the love between these men and women was greater than my love for my parishioners. When a situation with a parishioner became highly difficult for me, I could walk away – plead that I had to go tend to someone else who needed my immediate help. But Pete, a parishioner whose wife had terminal cancer couldn't walk away from that, make some excuse for leaving. Their love bond, at least it seemed to me at the time, was greater than the love that connected me to my parishioners.

It took me two years to make a decision. I prayed about it, worried about it, cried about it, talked to my bishop about it and sought help. I decided to get married, but my love for Jesus stayed the same. I took that with me. I'll always have Jesus.

One person that helped me significantly was my brother! Yes, Harmon, the brother who was always #1. The brother that, all my life, I was jealous of. My brother, Harmon, also was a priest. When I went to talk to him about my struggle, he was both receptive and wise. After several long conversations, he told me that I had to make my own decision but that he thought getting married would be a good choice. He reminded me that all through my life I followed him. He understood (although he had never mentioned this to me before) that in many ways I was always second to him. I followed him through eight years of grammar school. Every first day of school, my teacher would never say, "Oh, you're Joseph Skillin." She would instead say, "Oh, you're Harmon's little brother." He told me that! He continued enumerating that I followed him to the seminary for high school, because that was just the expectation. I followed him through four years of college, because that was the expectation. I followed him through four years post-grad in theology, because that was the expectation. Ever since we were little kids, I'd just follow my brother in school, one year behind him. After four years of theology, he was ordained a priest. After four years of theology, I was ordained a priest, expected, just one year behind him. His perception, his perspective, our conversations helped me make my decision.

The other person who encouraged me was Toots, my oldest sister, the one I always admired and enjoyed. "I always thought," she confided, "that you should be married."

Despite their encouragement, I still saw this as a difficult life choice. All this turmoil and struggle actually gave me the opportunity to rethink my life, rethink my Self in a different light. I was beginning to see now that I was OK, good, loved. And I didn't have to compare myself to anyone. I could accept who I was. I could be me, with self-confidence.

CHAPTER 15

A DIFFERENT PATH

THE DAY AFTER WE got married, my wife and I headed east from Oakland to Washington DC. My congressman had offered me a job in his Capitol office. It was an exhilarating time. Both marriage and work proved to be exciting, pleasant and fulfilling.

After a period of working for my congressman, I took a job with the Marriott Corporation, one of Washington's biggest employers. I had a lot to learn for both these jobs. My theological studies were not exactly designed to prepare me for government or big corporation employment. I tried to learn as quickly as possible and did pretty well at my jobs.

There was one specific experience that taught me a lesson about self-confidence. Fred Malek was one of the top executives in the Marriott Corporation. He also was a real presence in the politics, culture and social scene of D.C. He was my boss' boss. One day Mr. Malek offered me a different job within The Marriott Corporation. At the end of the discussion he stated that "if you stick with me, Joe, you'll be very happy and have an enormously successful life." I was honored and thrilled – for about a half hour.

Then I became insulted and angry. What? This man didn't think I could be happy and successful without riding his coat-tail? How insulting. The more I thought about it, the more insulted I was and the more angry I became. There was just something in his style and the way he blurted out that sugges-tion that he seemed to me more an arrogant manipulator than a kind boss who cared about me. I ignored the offer.

There was a positive aspect and a negative aspect to this inci-dent. On the positive side, I realized that I did not need this man to assure me a positive future. I realized that even though I was in a totally new stage of my life, I could succeed. Over the last few years I had grown in self-confidence. I still had my doubts, but by now my degree of self-confidence was gener-ally greater than the self-doubts. For me, this was significant progress.

The negative side of this incident pointed out clearly two de-ficiencies in me. The speed and determination of saying no to him highlighted my own proud stubbornness. If self-con-fidence is honestly accepting who I am, than I had to admit to pride and stubbornness, qualities I would need to change. I would need to craft two new affirmations to work on these problems.

Life went on.... a magnificent marriage to the most thought-ful and kind woman in the world, three bright, delightful kids whom I thoroughly enjoyed watching grow up, a family life filled with plenty of adventure, fun and love. Work was suc-cessful and my faith stayed strong.

After moving to Atlanta, I opened my own marketing and ad-vertising company. Life not only went on, but life was good. I continued successfully in my endeavors and appreciated ac-ceptance from many people, both friends and business associ-ates. I was better at accepting who I was, but still something seemed missing. Self-doubt was not completely gone. In es-sence, that wrestling match was still going on.

CHAPTER 16

BOTHERED BY PRIDE

I WAS HOOKED ON these affirmations from the beginning - *I like myself unconditionally* and *I am really happy being the unique and very special person that I am.* That ritual self-talk every morning and every evening enabled me to improve both internally and externally. A third affirmation that I added to my daily affirmations helped me internally – calming down, relaxing, reducing stress. Another helped me externally – starting my own business.

"I easily relax, as deeply as I wish, at any time" helped me significantly reduce my levels of worry. Starting my own business was a combination of need and opportunity. I wasn't making much money when we moved to Atlanta and I disliked the company I came here to work for. I began to stress a lot over the situation, so I deliberately ramped up that relaxing affirmation. When an opportunity presented itself, I opened my own small marketing/advertising company. If I had felt stress before, it could be an even bigger problem now. My own business! As my dad told me while we were looking at the Golden Gate bridge, I could get some help, but this was fully my responsibility. The relaxing affirmation helped me be prepared personally for this undertaking. Fortunately, with hard and smart work I made it a success. I was proud of that, satisfied both to do well and to provide well for my family. I accomplished this without undue stress, giving me the opportunity to be a relaxed person, generally pleasant, open and attentive to others, especially the family.

Life was good, everything fine. I felt I was king of the world, certainly king of my world. I could do almost anything, clearly everything I wanted to do. I could have it all and stay healthy to enjoy it all. Any problem was merely a minor blip. I was doing quite well, thank you. I liked myself and I was really comfortable being the unique and very special person that I am.

Then one day it hit me. How boastful! How arrogant! How proud! With all my success, with all my affirmations, with all my new-found confidence that I could accomplish so much, personally I was doing little more than growing in pride. Not the legitimate pride of satisfaction derived from my own qualities and achievements , but the selfish pride that set me apart from everyone else, the pride that actually isolated me from the world, the pride that puts me above all others, the boastful pride of self- importance and self-absorption.

I don't remember when this sense of arrogance hit me or where it came from. I don't recall any event that triggered it. But once I came to recognize this pride of arrogance, I had a new struggle. This self-absorbed attitude was completely contrary to what I was taught at home and at church. My mother and father never suggested that we be wimps, but neither did they teach us to be unduly proud. My dad was a huge success by anyone's standards. But he was a humble man and tried to teach all five of his children humility.

I was perplexed, bothered and unsure. All this work at trying to become self-confident, just to learn that I became no more than a proud man. Frustrating. There had to be an answer and I was determined to discover it.

CHAPTER 17

I LIKE MYSELF,
REVISED

RAISED A CATHOLIC, EDUCATED in Catholic schools even through post-grad years, ordained a priest, always staying connected to my religion, I finally came to the point of rethinking my self-confidence in light of my religion and personal upbringing.

I sensed validity in the affirmation "I like myself". Clearly, as an affirmation, it was founded on credible psychology. Pragmatically, it had helped me succeed over the years. It made sense to me to rethink this affirmation and reshape it rather than completely abandon it. I started thinking about three topics all at once: liking myself, self-confidence and a single, fundamental belief of my faith – creation. Eventually these three thoughts led to a single and simple conclusion for me: *If God created me, I should like myself and be self-confident.*

Statistically, most readers of this book come from a family raised at some point in an Abrahamic religion, including Judaism, Christianity and Islam. I am presuming, therefore, that most of my readers are familiar with the belief that man is created by God. We often hear the expression "going back to my maker" – spoken in movies and real life. Exactly. God is our maker to whom we will return when we die. I certainly believe that. It is that belief that changed my "like myself" – selfish and self-absorbed – to "like my Self".

I like my SELF unconditionally.

There is a difference between "myself" and "my Self". "Myself" is casual, usually focusing on what I have, what I've accomplished, what I want. It is all about the surface, the external, the temporal. And it has a selfish (root word self) connotation. I did this myself. I bought this for myself. I'm going to treat myself to a day at the spa. Myself also has a sneaky connotation of comparison. "I like myself" can be just one step away from, "But do I like you?" Comparisons, judgements, categorizing.

"my Self", however, is solely about me. No room for comparisons. It looks to my soul, my core, my inner being, my Me. My Self is what God created. The Bible describes creation as God forming me with his own two hands and then breathing into me his own life. That is awesome! It is not a question of whether or not you believe that literally. It is a question of whether you can believe the significance of the Genesis story. Mankind has always asked where we come from. All cultures, peoples, races ask that question and offer a collective answer, the most common answer being a creator.

If you are looking for self-confidence, it is reasonable to spend time contemplating the meaning of "Self". Start with Self. Then you will move to confidence. Self is that sacred being, You, placed into the midst of all creation. Self is not just an accidental you roaming alone through the world. Self is you created by God. Self is you deliberately chosen to be placed in this world by The Creator, however you define that. Deliberate. You are not an accident. Self, *your* Self, is not an accident.

Once you understand this, understand that you were deliberately created in the image of God, you have to appreciate your Self. As a friend told me, "God doesn't create any rejects." So see your Self as awesome, wonderful, magnificent. There is no reason to compare your Self to others. Just focus on where you came from and what you are -- hand made by God, filled essentially with his life. That Self you can accept and like for who you are. That's a Self you can be confident in.

This change in the affirmation gave me new perspective. The rewrite moved me from a cocky conviction that I was great to an honest appreciation for the awesome Me that God chose to create, a deep respect for this person I call My SELF.

When I like myself, I imply that I like myself even with all my faults and imperfections. When I like my SELF, I imply that I like my Self with all the beauty, dignity and power that God breathed into my soul, my core, my *me*.

Right after the Omega Seminar, "I like myself unconditionally" apparently started building my confidence. However, "I like my SELF", that simple but essential change, has enabled me to acquire not *apparent* but *true and authentic* self-confidence over the last twenty-five or thirty years. This Self, created by God, I truly like. I have utter confidence in this Self that God chose to create. I am comfortable with this Self. I trust this Self. The very definition of self-confidence

You can start now, building your own true, authentic, life-changing self-confidence by quietly and deliberately repeating several times daily, "I like my SELF, unconditionally."

CHAPTER 18

THE UNIQUE AND VERY SPECIAL PERSON, REVISED

THAT SECOND KEY AFFIRMATION from The Omega Seminar stated, "I am really comfortable being the unique and very special person that I am." This affirmation is meant to counter the universal tendency to self-doubt. Mr. Boyle spent two hours convincing us that most people doubt themselves, even if they act otherwise. He gave dozens of examples he learned from talking personally to famous people he had met – successful actors, politicians, business executives and academicians. Each person told Mr. Boyle his own story about self-doubt despite his or her many successes.

This is exactly what Nouwen meant when he described original sin as "humanity's endless capacity for self-rejection". This is exactly what Brené Brown means when she describes how we constantly think, "I am not enough." We have such a difficult time accepting ourselves for who we are.

And this is exactly what Joe Skillin was living for years, success without self-confidence. I was living with an endless capacity for self-rejection. I was living constantly believing I was not enough. No matter what success I had in life, I didn't have my brother's brains. No matter the level of personal success I found any time in my life, I still never heard those friends of my parents applaud when I gave my little talks. No matter how many people praised my wedding sermon, my brother was more handsome with black, shiny hair. Why did I keep these memories? Why did I hang on to these comparisons? How could I stop this self-defeat, this self-doubt?

I realized I had to change another affirmation.

Once I believe, in my own way, that I was created by God, I should like myself. I will appreciate myself. I will respect myself and try to show that respect in my daily living. It stands to reason and logic that if I like and appreciate myself, I should be fully satisfied just being the unique and very special person I am, the person God created. Essentially and existentially, that should be enough. One doesn't need diversions, external freedoms, riches, fun and self-comedy to be happy. Appreciation of God and Self are sufficient, as evidenced by many mystics throughout history. They radiated joy and happiness while having little in the way of accomplishment.

That second of Boyles' key affirmations, "I am really comfortable being the unique and very special person that I am", helped me to become more at ease with myself, despite my doubts. I was OK. I was happy with myself and becoming more comfortable with my Self. I was special and unique, so I was happy. I was unique in my upbringing, my education, my work, my accomplishments. Hey, everyone, I'm Joe Skillin – smart, decent looking, affable, a business success, have a great family, nice house...... Look at me! Yes, I'm happy, unique, very special. Look what I've accomplished for myself.

Wow. This was the second affirmation that went from good to utter conceit. Telling myself every day that I'm really happy being the unique and very special person that I am became self-absorbed conceit. Again, how boastful! How arrogant! How proud! I was unique and became very special by my own skills and hard work, so it seemed.

Realizing how this affirmation was feeding my conceit, I knew I had to change this one also. As written, it wasn't truly helping my self-confidence. It was, rather, merely allowing me to pat myself on the back for any and everything I accomplished.

Parallel to the change in my first affirmation, I changed the second affirmation to:

I am really comfortable being the unique and very special person that God created.

God created me *me*. He didn't create me as my brother Harmon. He didn't create me with neat, shiny black hair. He didn't create me with his slender body. No, he created me as my own single, separate, individual, different, unique, particular, distinct, specific Joseph Skillin. I'm the only me that God created. I'm the only Joe Skillin, born and raised in San Francisco, with four siblings, educated in the seminary for twelve years counting high school, ordained a priest, worked for my congressman from Contra Costa County, married to Penny Navone, business owner, author with a unique scar on my chin and three others around my face. That's me. No one else is me. I'm no one else. God created me unique.

Having come to realize that I am unique and special not because of what I have accomplished, but because God created me who I am, I can realize that I am enough. I don't need to return constantly to self-doubt. I count. I am me because God created me me. That is who I am and I can accept that. I **do** accept that. Thus, finally, I have come to accept who I am and find true Self-confidence.

It is not just that I am a unique person. Also, I am very special. I'm not very special in the sense of better than, superior to or having more importance than others. Rather, I am very special because God created me – no comparisons to anyone else. Just the simple fact that He created me makes me a special person, a very special person.

Unique and special, I have a life to live. What I do, how I live, what I accomplish, how popular I am is completely secondary to the unique and special SELF that God created. The road to true self-confidence is deep within each of us. It is accepting,

in your very core, that God made you, that He made you unique
and special.

CHAPTER 19

FINALLY, I LIKE MY SELF

YEARS AGO, I FINALLY realized that I was not *created* with self-doubt. From my earliest years, I *became* self-doubting in an environment of negative words, comparisons and judgments.

It took me many years, many, to learn that I need not doubt my Self, to fully realize I was created good, special, worthy of life, wonderful.

Today, I've come to accept honestly who I am and not worry much about accomplishment and popularity. Are they important to me? Clearly I like them and probably too often seek them. But they are background now. What counts is the knowledge that

I like my SELF unconditionally and

I am really comfortable being the unique and very special person that God created.

Simply stated ...... Finally, I like my Self.

POINTS TO REMEMBER #3

1. There is a difference between what you accomplish and who you are.

2. Self-repeated negative thoughts keep you negative.

3. Self-repeated positive affirmations help improve your skills.

4. Two special, self-repeated affirmations * improve your Self-confidence.

5. Do not confuse popularity and Self-confidence.

6. Do not confuse pride and Self-confidence.

7. You are a unique and very special person.

* I like my SELF unconditionally and I am really comfortable being the unique and very special person that God created.

WHAT IS SELF-CONFIDENCE?

- CHAPTER 21 -

WHAT SELF-CONFIDENCE IS NOT

You can be a star, the very best, but be without self-confidence. A good example of someone who exhibited excellence without self-confidence is Johnny Manziel, Johnny Football.

At Texas A&M, he scored and soared, destined to be the best of today and tomorrow. He racked up a laundry list of NCAA and SEC records. He became the first freshman to win the Heisman Trophy. Then, so his story goes, drafted by the Cleveland Browns, Johnny struggled with on-field mediocrity and off-field personal problems. Drinking, carousing, gambling, some say drugs, booked into and out of the Highland Park jail for domestic violence. Finally cut by the Browns after two years. What a crash! His life seemed like a deflated balloon when he had nothing to do but just go back to school.

Why didn't his on-field confidence help him to continue his college success? Because he didn't have SELF-confidence. All he had was confidence in his ability to play football. Later, that confidence was overwhelmed by a terrible lifestyle.

We see this today with many athletes, for example in the NFL. Outstanding football players who have a high degree of confidence in their ability to play football, but little Self-confidence. Deep in their core, they don't like themselves very much, are not happy being the special persons that God created. Their confidence is only in a personal skill. Without Self-confidence, some of them, troubled, easily fall to violence and crime.

Hollywood is another arena of people successful in acting but shallow in Self-confidence. They are confident in what they do but not in who they are. They keep struggling to repeat the "do" while unable to like the "who". Their upside down life makes them self-absorbed or bitter or arrogant or entitled. "If I can just protect my public persona, I'll always like myself." As opposed to liking Self because of accepting who you are, not what you've done.

Some people mistake popularity for Self-confidence. If so many people like Pete, the thinking goes, he must really be a confident guy. I can attest to the fact that neither achievement nor popularity equal self-confidence. Nor are they a sure sign of it. Remember when I was in school, on the Campus Crew, on the swim team, a good public speaker? These talents, achievements did not translate into Self-confidence. When I was pastor of the cathedral, standing on the church steps greeting people who were lauding my sermon, I stood in self-doubt, uncomfortably seeking a way to leave and go back to the solitude of the rectory.

Self-confidence is not achievement or popularity. Achievement and popularity are external. Self-confidence is internal, deep in your core, in your soul.

CHAPTER 22

WHY ARE PEOPLE NOT SELF-CONFIDENT?

WHEN I WAS IN the first grade, I dreaded getting my Report Card and brining it home. I remember my very first report – a few A's, but also two C's. My first thought was that it wasn't as good as my brother's report card. Then, the thought became that *I* was not as good as my brother.

When I got home and gave the card to my mother, she made some comment about C's not being very good. Then she voiced, what in those days was so common a statement/warning/threat: Just wait until your father gets home. Gulp. So when he got home, said hello, everybody got their hug or kiss, my mother presented him with the card. "C's? You have to do better than that. Your brother didn't get any C's. Neither did your sisters."

Comparison. *De facto* and implied. You got C's and they did not. Implied, at least slightly, is a statement that *I* was not as good as them. My dad was referring to my lack of ability in school. I transposed it from school work to my Self.

I believe we are born with basic self-confidence. It's the way we were created – special, magnificent, wonderful. But early on, very early, belief in that innate self-confidence is shattered by words of insufficiency. From an early age, we are trained by our loving, influencing parents to question that confidence. Through their directives (words, gestures, actions) we are compared to others. Then, like good children, we learn from them and take to ourselves the task of comparison. Always comparisons. It becomes difficult to accept who I am if I believe someone else is better than I am.

Another way we rob ourselves from that innate Self-confidence is by moving from comparison to feelings such as I am not enough, I don't fit well with this group, I don't belong here. When we compare ourselves to others, we separate ourselves. First we categorize: them and me. Then we define: them and me. Then we grade: them and me. Then we judge: them and me. All this comparing, grading and judging pushes us into serious self-doubt. No, I'm not as good. No, I can't compete on that level. No, I'm not enough. No, I don't fit in. The more we doubt, the more we speed the downward spiral of applying self-doubt to every aspect of life. I'm not smart enough becomes I'm not smart. I'm not pretty enough becomes I'm not pretty. I'm not comfortable enough becomes I'm not comfortable. And, the worst, I'm not good enough becomes I'm not good.

Our comparisons lead to self-doubt. Self-doubt is poison and keeps us from acquiring a healthy degree of Self-confidence.

CHAPTER 23

WHAT IS SELF-CONFIDENCE?

Self-confidence is accepting myself for who I am.

Self-confidence is a deep, internal happiness knowing I am unique and very special.

Self-confidence is a complete void of the need to compare myself to others.

Self-confidence is a deeply spiritual conviction that I am enough.

Self-confidence is a deep-seated liking for this Self, me, that God created.

Self-confidence is a permeating comfort with this Self, me, that God created.

Does Self-confidence mean you are perfect? No. There is a difference between *who you are at your core* and *what you achieve or accomplish*. You will still make poor judgements at times. You are not perfect, even though you are special and unique. You will still get angry, irritated or frustrated at times. You will make mistakes. You will fail in some of your efforts. You will always have room to improve what you do and how you behave. But your core, your created You, is stand-alone good, with no need for comparisons, always worthy of acceptance, sufficient in magnificence. Despite your imperfections, you are worthy of love and belonging.

Does Self-confidence mean you can accomplish and excel at anything? No. As one can have a highly developed skill without real self-confidence, so one can have true Self-confidence without certain skills. Self-confidence does not mean you won't fail at various activities. It does not mean you won't be afraid to try new things. Again, the skills, disciplines, virtues you try to develop are external. Self-confidence is internal.

While Self-confidence, in itself, does not equate to skill-confidence, it does help one succeed in life. If you appreciate the fact that God created you as a unique and very special person, you will respect yourself and be open to chasing new endeavors – because you sense, deep down, that you are capable. This feeling will not be universal. There will be things you just don't have any interest in, tasks you don't care to try, challenges you are reluctant to try. Sensing that you are unique and special, however, what you do decide to attempt, will probably be successful.

Does being self-confident get you an Outstanding on Life's report card? No. You are not better than any other person. Maybe more skills, but not better as a created person. You are not above others. Maybe more material possessions, but not better as a person. Maybe more accomplishments, medals, awards and fame, but not better as a person.

Self-confidence is liking your Self, your inner being, your core that God created, unconditionally.

Self-confidence is being really comfortable as the unique and very special person that God created.

Like your Self.

Be comfortable with your uniqueness and specialness.

Be Self-confident.

CHAPTER 24

HOW DOES ONE ACHIEVE SELF-CONFIDENCE?

My answer to this question comes from my own experience. In sum, there are two steps essential to achieving Self-confidence.

Get rid of The Opposition.

Correctly affirm your Self-confidence.

Opposition. The Opposition is the sum of all that self-doubt I mentioned throughout this book. It's your opponent in the everlasting wrestling match I've described. Deeply held negative thoughts about our insufficiency are a barrier to Self-confidence. Negative thoughts, negative self-beliefs can come from either our childhood or more recent life incidents. The old childhood beliefs are the hardest to recall, to recognize and to overcome. Old or recent, I call them The Opposition.

When my brother was about 45 years old, we were talking frankly one afternoon about family – the good and the not so good. At one point he related a childhood story in which our dad called him Dizzy. Then my dad continued to use that nick-name for years. "That hurt," cried (literally) my brother. "And it still hurts. It still affects me. I'm not Dizzy and he shouldn't have called me that." I responded harshly, "Hey. How old are you? Let it go! Get over it!" End of conversation.

While insensitive in the manner I handled this revelation, I be-lieve I was correct in my assessment. He had been harboring this put-down for dozens of years, keeping it in his thoughts, using it as an excuse for any problem in his life. "It still af-fects me." The worst effect of holding this thought and feeling was that it built within my brother significant self-doubt. My brother, a seeming success in his life, whom I always believed to be self-confident, had a paralyzing case of self-doubt.

We all have lived similar stories. We have all been called nega-tive names, inadvertently or deliberately insulted by our par-ents, told we are not good, not able, not capable. Then we hold on to those denials, surely in our sub-conscious, sometimes in our conscious state. Everything negative that has been crowd-ed into our minds over our years of living is The Opposition, building barriers to Self-confidence.

The first step to achieve Self-confidence is to rid yourself of The Opposition. Recognize what you can of your personal Opposition. You were not *created* with self-doubt. You were created good, special, worthy of life, wonderful. Then from your earliest years, you *became* self-doubting in an environment of negative words, comparisons and judgments.

Shaming, comparisons, bullying, denials, they all hurt when they originally happened. But you don't need to keep them, harbor them, repeat them. These are The Opposition. They happened in the past. Essentially they were external. They were unfair, unnecessary comparisons and judgements. They never were descriptions of the deep, core, magnificent, beautiful YOU that God created. Recognize The Opposition for what it is. Let it go.

Then you are free to take the second step to achieve Self-confidence: affirm it.

As said earlier, affirmations are mental tools. The affirmation statement you repeat in your mind changes your self-belief. If you affirm negatively, you self-believe negatively, doubt yourself. If you affirm positively, you self-believe positively. Positive affirmations have helped me achieve personal, spiritual and tangible goals. And they have made me Self-confident. They will, also, for you.

When I first learned of affirmations, I repeated every day those two basic statements: I like myself unconditionally and I am really happy being the unique and very special person that I am. They eventually affected a change in me, but a change I was not proud of – pride. They made me feel superior. I became judgmental with quietly cocky, arrogant self-absorption that made me think I was better than everyone else. They made me compare, rank and judge. I thought they were making me self-confident, but, fortunately, I finally realized they were not.

It was only years later that I changed those two original affirmations to statements of true Self-appreciation and Self-confidence. It was only when I changed those two affirmations to support an acceptance of who I am at my core that I began to develop true Self-confidence. It was only when I changed those two affirmations to remove all sense of comparison, unworthiness and judgement hidden within them that I began to develop true Self-confidence.

You will develop Self-confidence by affirming, by telling yourself every day, by repeating to yourself every day:

I like my SELF unconditionally.

I am really comfortable being the unique and very special person that God created.

The most effective way to "do your affirmations" is to repeat them every morning and every night. We were taught to make these two affirmations such a priority that we should do them first thing when we woke up. Sit on the edge of the bed. Close your eyes. Take a few slow breaths. Then, with deliberate concentration, repeat each affirmation five times. At night, just before you go to sleep, sit on the edge of your bed. Close your eyes. Take a few slow breaths. Then, with deliberate concentration, repeat each affirmation five times. Every morning. Every night. Every day. Affirming is not just an action. It is a way of living.

Go back and re-read chapters 17 and 18 to refresh your understanding of what these two affirmations mean. Then just start repeating them again and again and again until they become you and you become them. You will come to the point that you *know* these two statements, not just *say* them. They work. They will change you. It will take time, but you will become Self-confident. It is gradual. It is a 'becomingness". Imperceptibly day by day, slightly noticeable month by month. It's a process. It needs time and work. But put in the time and work, because you are special and unique and you deserve to fully recognize that about yourself. You deserve to be comfortable with your Self, trust your Self, like your Self.

And I say that with absolute confidence!

JOSEPH SKILLIN
January 24, 2021

CPSIA information can be obtained
at www.ICGtesting.com
Printed in the USA
LVHW031122060521
686680LV00008B/386